A CHILDREN BOOK
OF
MOTIVATION &
INSPIRATION
AGES 8 & UP

"DID YOU KNOW"
"DID YOU"

BY
MARVIN MILLER

iUniverse, Inc.
New York   Bloomington

iUniverse books may be ordered through booksellers or by contacting:

iUniverse
1663 Liberty Drive
Bloomington, IN 47403
www.iuniverse.com
1-800-Authors (1-800-288-4677)

Because of the dynamic nature of the Internet, any Web addresses or links contained in this book may have changed since publication and may no longer be valid. The views expressed in this work are solely those of the author and do not necessarily reflect the views of the publisher, and the publisher hereby disclaims any responsibility for them.

ISBN: 978-1-4502-4656-9 (sc)
ISBN: 978-1-4502-4657-6 (ebook)

Printed in the United States of America

iUniverse rev. date: 07/20/2010

HELLO BOYS AND GIRLS OF THE
WORLD. HOW ARE YOU TODAY ? I HOPE
YOU'RE ALL DOING GOOD AND THAT YOU'RE
HAVING A GOOD DAY. MY NAME IS MARVIN
MILLER AND PLEASE ALLOW ME TO ASK
YOU A FEW QUESTIONS, O.K.! I KNOW KIDS
OF THE WORLD TODAY, ARE SMARTER, THAN
THEY WHERE WHEN I WAS A KID. I KNOW
YOU'LL BE ABLE TO UNDERSTAND, THE FEW
THINGS I WOULD LIKE TO KNOW; SO HERE
WE GO WITH, DID YOU KNOW, DID YOU?

DID YOU KNOW, GOD MADE YOU TO BE SPECIAL ? DID YOU KNOW, GOD LOVES YOU ? DID YOU KNOW, GOD WAKES YOU UP EVERYDAY, BECAUSE HE LOVES YOU, AND WANTS YOU TO HAVE A GOOD DAY ? DID YOU KNOW, DID YOU ?

DID YOU KNOW, SOME OF US HAVE

FATHERS AT HOME AND SOME OF US DON'T ?

DID YOU KNOW SOME OF US LIVE WITH OUR

GRAND-PARENTS, UNCLES AND AUNTS ?

SOME OF US LIVE IN FOSTER HOMES, BUT

GOD NEVER LEAVES US ALONE. GOD GIVES

US ALL A HOME. DID YOU KNOW, DID YOU ?

DID YOU KNOW, GOD WANTS US TO
RESPECT OUR FATHER AND MOTHER AND
TO LOVE ONE ANOTHER AND TO BE NICE
TO YOUR SISTER OR BROTHER ? DID YOU
KNOW IF WE ALL GOT ALONG, WE WOULD
ALL HAVE HAPPY HOMES ? DID YOU KNOW,
DID YOU ?

DID YOU KNOW, A SMILE IS LIKE

SUNSHINE, IT WILL BRIGHTEN SOME-ONES

DAY. THEY MAY BE FEELING SAD AND IT

WAS YOUR SMILE, THAT HELP THEM GET

THROUGH THE DAY. I TOLD YOU, YOU

WERE SPECIAL. DID YOU KNOW, DID YOU ?

DID YOU KNOW, WHEN YOU'RE NICE

TO SOMEONE, THEY'LL APPRECIATE YOU

MORE ? DID YOU KNOW WHEN YOU TALK

AND SAY NICE THINGS, PEOPLE WILL

NOTICE WHAT YOU HAVE TO SAY. YOU ARE

IMPORTANT AND SO ARE YOUR THOUGHTS.

DID YOU KNOW DID YOU?

DID YOU KNOW, WHEN YOU'RE

COURTEOUS TO PEOPLE AND YOU BE POLITE

IT'S A REFLECTION OF YOUR PARENTS AND

IT TELLS PEOPLE THEY'RE RAISING YOU RIGHT

AND IT MAKES EVERYONE LOOK RIGHT.

THAT'S WHY IT'S SO IMPORTANT TO BE NICE.

DID YOU KNOW, DID YOU ?

DID YOU KNOW, YOUR PARENTS ONLY
WANT WHAT'S BEST FOR YOU, SIMPLY
BECAUSE THEY LOVE YOU. SOMETIMES
THEY MAY DO THINGS YOU DON'T
UNDERSTAND, BUT AS YOU GET OLDER
YOU'LL SEE AND UNDERSTAND A LOT MORE
AND REALIZE THE LESSON THEY WERE
TRYING TO SHOW YOU. DID YOU KNOW,
DID YOU ?

DID YOU KNOW, ALL OF YOUR DREAMS

CAN BECOME YOUR REALITY. IF YOU

STRIVE HARD, YOU CAN ACCOMPLISH

ANYTHING. BELIEVE IN YOURSELF

BECAUSE, THERE'S NOTHING, YOU CAN'T

DO. DID YOU KNOW, JUST HOW SPECIAL

YOU ARE ? DID YOU KNOW, DID YOU ?

DID YOU KNOW, EVERYTHING HAS A

PRICE, THERE'S CONSEQUENCE'S FOR

EVERYONE'S ACTIONS, SO TRY TO ALWAYS

THINK, BEFORE YOU REACT TO SOMETHING,

AND IT WILL SAVE YOU FROM GETTING

IN TROUBLE. DID YOU KNOW, DID YOU ?

DID YOU KNOW, EVEN THOUGH YOU

LEARN A LOT FROM YOUR PARENTS, THEY

ALSO LEARN A LOT FROM YOU. SELF

MOTIVATION, WILL PUSH YOU TO THE TOP

AND ALONG THE WAY, IF YOU FALL, IT'S

O.K., BECAUSE YOU CAN DO ANYTHING.

DID YOU KNOW, DID YOU ?

DID YOU KNOW, IT'S O.K. TO TRY TO

DO THINGS ON YOUR OWN, IT'S O.K. IF

SOMETHING GOES WRONG, BECAUSE YOU

CAN ALWAYS TRY AGAIN, YOU'LL

EVENTUALLY GET IT RIGHT. PLUS, YOU CAN

ALWAYS DEPEND ON YOUR PARENTS.

DID YOU KNOW, DID YOU ?

DID YOU KNOW, IT'S NOT GOOD TO

HOLD STUFF INSIDE. FIND SOMEONE YOU

CAN EXPRESS YOUR FEELINGS TO AND

SHARE YOUR THOUGHTS WITH. DID YOU

KNOW, YOU CAN ALWAYS GO TO YOUR

PARENTS WITH YOUR PROBLEMS ?

DID YOU KNOW, DID YOU ?

DID YOU KNOW, WHEN YOU'RE CURIOUS

ABOUT THINGS, THAT'S GOOD, IT'S

ANOTHER WAY TO LEARN. THERE'S NO

SUCH THING AS A STUPID QUESTION

AND WHEN YOU NEED THE ANSWER TO

SOMETHING, DON'T HESITATE TO ASK,

O.K.. DID YOU KNOW, DID YOU ?

DID YOU KNOW, WHEN YOU EAT RIGHT,

GET YOUR PROPER REST AND EXERCISE,

YOUR TAKING GOOD CARE OF YOUR

HEALTH AND YOU WILL LIVE LONGER.

NOBODY BUT GOD CAN LOVE YOU MORE

THAN YOU LOVE YOURSELF. DID YOU KNOW

DID YOU ?

DID YOU KNOW, IF YOU EAT A BALANCED

BREAKFAST, BEFORE YOU GO TO SCHOOL,

YOU WILL BE ABLE TO CONCENTRATE

BETTER AND LUNCH TIME WILL COME

BEFORE YOU KNOW IT ? DID YOU KNOW,

DID YOU ?

DID YOU KNOW, HARD WORK ALWAYS
PAYS OFF, TO ACHIEVE ANYTHING THAT'S
WORTH YOUR WHILE, YOU HAVE TO WORK
TO GET IT AND WHEN YOU GET IT YOU
WILL APPRECIATE IT MORE AND IT WILL
MEAN MORE TO YOU. DID YOU KNOW,
DID YOU ?

DID YOU KNOW, PEOPLE WHO GET A

COLLEGE EDUCATION, MAKE MORE

MONEY, HAVE NICE CARS, LIVE IN BIG

HOUSES. REMEMBER THE MORE YOU READ

THE MORE YOU'LL KNOW AND YOUR MIND

WILL GROW. DID YOU KNOW, DID YOU ?

DID YOU KNOW, WHEN YOU DO

SOMETHING THAT'S WRONG, IT'S BEST

TO TELL THE TRUTH, YOUR PARENTS

MAY GET MAD, BUT THEY'LL LEARN

THEY CAN TRUST YOU AND THEY WILL

RESPECT YOU. REMEMBER, HONESTY IS THE

BEST POLICY. DID YOU KNOW, DID YOU ?

DID YOU KNOW, WHEN YOU THINK

POSITIVE, YOUR ACTIONS WILL BECOME

POSITIVE AND YOU'LL GET POSITIVE

RESULTS THAT WILL SET YOU ON A

POSITIVE PATH, TO THE ROAD OF SUCCESS,

BECAUSE YOU ARE SPECIAL, YOU'RE THE

BEST. DID YOU KNOW, DID YOU ?

DID YOU KNOW, YOU CAN GET IN

TROUBLE WHEN YOU DO BAD THINGS,

SO TRY TO DO GOOD. TROUBLE IS EASY

TO GET INTO AND SOMETIMES IT'S SO

HARD TO GET OUT OF, SO REMEMBER

TO ALWAYS THINK BEFORE YOU REACT.

DID YOU KNOW, DID YOU ?

DID YOU KNOW, IF YOU STUDY HARD, YOU CAN BE GOOD IN SCHOOL. IF YOU PRACTICE HARD, YOU CAN BE GOOD IN SPORTS. NEVER QUIT NO MATTER HOW HARD IT GETS, KEEP TRYING, UNTIL YOU GET IT, BECAUSE YOU ARE GREAT. DID YOU KNOW, DID YOU ?

DID YOU KNOW, WHEN YOU BEEN

WORKING FOR A LONG TIME, IF YOU TAKE

OUT THE TIME TO RELAX YOUR MIND, IT

WILL MAKE YOU FEEL BETTER, THINK

BETTER AND CONCENTRATE ON YOUR

HOMEWORK BETTER, BECAUSE YOU ARE

VERY SMART. DID YOU KNOW, DID YOU?

DID YOU KNOW, YOU HAVE THE

POTENTIAL TO BE GREAT AND BECOME

ANYTHING YOU WANT TO BE. NEVER

TELL YOURSELF YOU CAN'T BECAUSE

YOU CAN DO ANYTHING YOU SET YOUR

MIND TO. YOU ARE VERY SPECIAL AND

YOU CAN DO ANYTHING. DID YOU KNOW,

DID YOU?

DID YOU KNOW, IF YOU DON'T PUT YOUR MIND TO USE, IT WILL GO TO WASTE. THINK BIG AND SET BIG GOALS, STARTING WITH ONE STEP AT A TIME, UNTIL YOU GET THERE. THERE IS NO LIMIT ON HOW FAR YOU CAN GO. DID YOU KNOW, DID YOU?

DID YOU KNOW, TO NEVER BE AFRAID

TO BE YOURSELF, TRUE COURAGE COMES

FROM NOT BEING AFRAID TO BE DIFFERENT,

YOU'RE ORIGINAL, YOU'RE ONE OF A KIND,

YOU'RE VERY SPECIAL, YOU ARE UNIQUE.

DID YOU KNOW, DID YOU?

DID YOU KNOW, IDLE TIME IS THE
DEVILS WORK SHOP, SO USE YOUR TIME
DOING POSITIVE THINGS AND IT WILL KEEP
YOU OUT OF TROUBLE, REMEMBER THAT I
TOLD YOU, TROUBLE IS EASY TO GET INTO
AND HARD TO GET OUT OF. DID YOU KNOW,
DID YOU ?

DID YOU KNOW, YOUR PARENTS DON'T
WANT YOU TO MAKE THE SAME MISTAKES
THEY MADE, THEY WANT YOU TO BE BETTER
THEN THEM, SO PAY ATTENTION TO WHAT
THEY SAY BECAUSE THEY BEEN WHERE
YOU'RE TRYING TO GO AND IF YOU LISTEN,
YOU WILL DO BETTER THEN THEY DID.
DID YOU KNOW, DID YOU?

DID YOU KNOW, IF YOU'RE ASHAMED TO

TELL SOMEONE WHAT YOU DID, THEN

DON'T DO IT. NO MATTER WHAT ANYONE

THINKS OF YOU, YOU ARE A VERY

IMPORTANT PERSON, NEVER ALLOW

ANYONE'S NEGATIVE OPINION OF YOU

TO BECOME YOUR REALITY. DID YOU KNOW,

DID YOU?

DID YOU KNOW, IF OTHER KIDS TRY TO

TALK YOU INTO DOING SOMETHING THAT

YOU KNOW IS NOT RIGHT, IT'S CALLED

PEER PRESSURE AND THAT IS THE MOMENT

YOU SHOULD BECOME A LEADER AND NOT

A FOLLOWER. A REAL FRIEND WILL NEVER

LEAD YOU TO TROUBLE. DID YOU KNOW,

DID YOU?

DID YOU KNOW, IF ANYONE EVER

TOUCH YOUR PRIVATE PARTS, OR TOUCH

YOU IN A WAY THAT MAKES YOU FEEL

UNCOMFORTABLE, THEN TRY TO TRICK

YOU INTO NOT TELLING ANYONE, TELL

YOUR PARENTS OR YOUR TEACHER ON

THEM ANYWAY, THEY WILL HELP YOU

AND PROTECT YOU. DID YOU KNOW,

DID YOU?

DID YOU KNOW, YOU SHOULD ALWAYS SAY NO TO TOBACCO, ALCOHOL, DRUGS AND GANGS. IF YOU ARE OFFERED THESE THINGS IN YOUR NEIGHBORHOOD, PLAYGROUND OR SCHOOL, TELL THEM NO, BECAUSE YOU'RE TOO COOL TO BE A FOOL. DID YOU KNOW, DID YOU?

DID YOU KNOW, THE DICTIONARY IS

FULL OF KNOWLEDGE AND INFORMATION,

LOOK UP THE WORDS, INTEGRITY, MORALS,

DIGNITY, HONOR AND PROSPERITY. WAIT,

DO THE DICTIONARY KNOW YOU; BECAUSE

THOSE WORDS SHOULD DESCRIBE YOU.

DID YOU KNOW, DID YOU?

DID YOU KNOW, ALMOST ALL ATHLETES

IN PRO SPORTS WENT TO COLLEGE. IF YOU

LIKE SPORTS AND HAVE DREAMS OF GOING

TO THE PROS ONE DAY, STUDY HARD IN

SCHOOL AND THE COLLEGE DOORS WILL

BE OPEN TO YOU. DID YOU KNOW, DID YOU?

DID YOU KNOW, IDEAS MAKE PEOPLE

RICH. WHEN YOU GET A GOOD IDEA WRITE

IT DOWN. THE WORLDS BEST INVENTIONS

STARTED AS SOMEONE'S IDEAS. LOTS OF

INVENTIONS CAME FROM KIDS? DID YOU

KNOW, DID YOU?

DID YOU KNOW, YOUR ATTITUDE TELLS

PEOPLE A LOT ABOUT YOU. IT CAN ALSO BE

THE FACTOR TO DECIDE HOW FAR YOU CAN

GO IN LIFE, SO KEEP A GOOD ATTITUDE AND

REACH FOR THE STARS. REMEMBER THERE'S

NO LIMIT ON HOW FAR YOU CAN GO. DID

YOU KNOW, DID YOU?

DID YOU KNOW, MATH WILL OPEN THE
DOOR, FOR ALL KINDS OF JOB
OPPORTUNITIES, SO DON'T BE SCARED TO
CHALLENGE YOUR MIND, BECAUSE WHEN
YOU STUDY AND REALLY TRY HARD, YOU
CAN FIGURE ANYTHING OUT, YOUR BRAIN
IS POWERFUL. DID YOU KNOW, DID YOU?

DID YOU KNOW, YOU SHOULD ENJOY BEING A KID, DON'T BE IN A HURRY TO BECOME A GROWN-UP, MOST GROWN-UP'S WISH THEY COULD HAVE BEEN A KID A LITTLE LONGER. YOUR TOYS AND VIDEO GAMES ARE BETTER THEN THE TOYS WE HAD. DID YOU KNOW, DID YOU?

DID YOU KNOW, TO NEVER MAKE FUN OF SOMEONE, BECAUSE OF THE COLOR OF THEIR SKIN, HOW THEY LOOK OR BECAUSE THEY HAVE A HANDICAP; ALWAYS RESPECT PEOPLE AND YOU MUST ALWAYS RESPECT YOUR ELDERS. DID YOU KNOW, DID YOU?

DID YOU KNOW, AS YOU LIVE YOUR

DREAM OUT, LET NOTHING OR ANYTHING

STOP YOU. NEVER LISTEN TO THE PEOPLE

WHO SAY YOU CAN'T ACHIEVE SOMETHING,

MAYBE THEY CAN'T, BUT YOU CAN.

NOBODY CAN TAKE A EDUCATION FROM

YOU, ONCE YOU GET IT, IT'S YOURS TO

KEEP. DID YOU KNOW, DID YOU?

DID YOU KNOW, TO ALWAYS HAVE HIGH

SELF ESTEEM, YOU ARE THE BEST AND

NEVER LET ANYONE TELL YOU OTHERWISE.

ALWAYS CARRY YOURSELF WITH

CONFIDENCE, YOU ARE A LEADER, YOU

ARE SMART AND YOU ARE INTELLIGENT.

DID YOU KNOW, DID YOU?

DID YOU KNOW, THAT WHEN YOU START

SOMETHING, YOU SHOULD SEE IT THROUGH,

NO MATTER HOW HARD IT GETS NEVER

TELL YOURSELF, I CAN'T FINISH, YOU CAN,

YOU MUST ALWAYS PERSEVERE. YOU CAN

DO ANYTHING YOU PUT YOUR MIND TO.

DID YOU KNOW, DID YOU?

DID YOU KNOW, WHEN YOU TELL

YOUR PARENTS THEIR OLD FASHION,

THEY BE LAUGHING INSIDE, BECAUSE

THEY ONCE TOLD THEIR PARENTS THE SAME

THING; LISTEN AND PAY CLOSE ATTENTION

TO WHAT THEY HAVE TO SAY, THEY MAY

UNDERSTAND MORE THAN YOU REALIZE.

DID YOU KNOW, DID YOU?

DID YOU KNOW, YOU LEARN LESSONS FROM THE THINGS YOU GO THROUGH IN LIFE, SO PAY ATTENTION TO YOUR EXPERIENCE, SOME-THINGS YOU'LL REMEMBER AND SOME-THINGS WILL MAKE YOU REMEMBER THE HARD WAY. DID YOU KNOW, DID YOU?

DID YOU KNOW, THAT ALL THINGS

ARE POSSIBLE, ALWAYS HAVE THE POWER

TO VISUALIZE AND YOU CAN MAKE

ANYTHING HAPPEN, ALWAYS BELIEVE

IN YOURSELF, YOU CAN DO ANYTHING

YOU PUT YOUR MIND TO. YOU ARE A

WINNER. DID YOU KNOW, DID YOU?

DID YOU KNOW, WHEN SOMETHING IS

ON YOUR MIND, YOU SHOULD SPEAK UP,

YOU ARE A VERY IMPORTANT PERSON AND

WHAT YOU HAVE TO SAY IS IMPORTANT, SO

PLEASE SPEAK UP, WHAT YOU SAY, MAY

HELP SOMEONE. DID YOU KNOW, DID YOU?

DID YOU KNOW, WHEN YOU'RE LOOKING

GOOD, IT MAKES YOU FEEL GOOD ABOUT

YOURSELF, SO KEEP YOUR HYGIENE'S UP

AND YOURSELF UP TO THE BEST OF YOUR

ABILITY. EXERCISING WILL MAKE YOU

FEEL BETTER. DID YOU KNOW DID YOU?

DID YOU KNOW, TO ALWAYS BELIEVE IN

YOURSELF, EVEN WHEN YOU'RE FEELING

WEAK, BELIEVE IN YOUR STRENGTH.

GOD GAVE US ALL A TALENT AND ONCE

YOU FIND YOURS, YOU WILL BE THE

BEST AT IT. DID YOU KNOW, DID YOU?

DID YOU KNOW, EVEN THOUGH THINGS

MAY LOOK BAD TODAY, THEY WILL GET

BETTER TOMORROW. HAVE PATIENCE

AND THINGS WILL GET BETTER, THE

POSITIVE WILL COME OUT, THE BEST

IS YET TO COME. DID YOU KNOW, DID YOU?

DID YOU KNOW, IT'S GOOD TO ALWAYS

THINK POSITIVE? DON'T WAIT UNTIL YOU

GET PUT IN A SITUATION TO THINK, TRY

TO SEE IT COMING AND THINK YOUR WAY

THROUGH IT. YOU ARE VERY SMART.

DID YOU KNOW, DID YOU?

DID YOU KNOW, TO ALWAYS BE

YOURSELF. NEVER TRY TO BE SOMEONE

ELSE, YOU CAN NEVER BE THEM. GOD

MADE YOU UNIQUE, YOUR ONE OF A

KIND, SO LOVE YOURSELF AS YOU ARE,

YOU ARE SPECIAL. DID YOU KNOW, DID

YOU?

DID YOU KNOW, NOT TO BELIEVE

EVERYTHING YOU HEAR AND SEE ON T.V.

MOST OF THE ACTORS, DON'T LIVE OR ACT

LIKE THAT FOREAL, THAT'S WHY THEY CALL

IT ACTING, SO BE CAREFUL ON WHO YOU

TRY TO ACT LIKE. DID YOU KNOW, DID YOU?

DID YOU KNOW, IT'S NOT IMPORTANT WHAT OTHER PEOPLE THINK ABOUT YOU. WHAT IS IMPORTANT, IS WHAT YOU THINK OF YOURSELF. ALWAYS THINK HIGHLY OF YOURSELF FOR WHO YOU ARE, NOT FOR WHAT OTHERS WANT YOU TO BE. DID YOU KNOW, DID YOU?

DID YOU KNOW, WHAT YOU BELIEVE WILL EFFECT THE WAY YOU ACT. IF YOU BELIEVE YOU'RE A BAD PERSON, YOU'LL DO BAD THINGS. IF YOU BELIEVE YOU'RE A GOOD PERSON YOU'LL DO GOOD THINGS. YOU ALWAYS HAVE A CHOICE. IT'S YOUR DECISION. DID YOU KNOW, DID YOU?

DID YOU KNOW, THAT A SHIP THAT SITS

STILL WILL ROT, BUT IF YOU LET IT SAIL,

YOU WILL SEE GREAT THINGS AND GREAT

PLACES. A BRAIN THAT SITS STILL, WILL GO

TO WASTE, BUT IF YOU FEED IT WITH

KNOWLEDGE, IT WILL GROW AND DO

GREAT THINGS. DID YOU KNOW, DID YOU?

DID YOU KNOW, THAT ALL THINGS

COME TO PASS, SO WHATEVER YOUR

GOING THROUGH TODAY, NEVER GIVE

UP; THERE'S ALWAYS HOPE THAT

TOMORROW WILL BRING ABOUT A

CHANGE. THE BEST IS YET TO COME.

DID YOU KNOW, DID YOU?

DID YOU KNOW, TO NEVER GIVE UP

JUST BECAUSE YOU FAILED AT SOMETHING.

KEEP TRYING UNTIL YOU GET IT RIGHT,

IT WILL MEAN MORE TO YOU AND YOU'LL

APPRECIATE IT MORE. ALWAYS KEEP TRYING,

YOU'LL GET IT RIGHT. DID YOU KNOW,

DID YOU?

DID YOU KNOW, NOTHING IS AS BAD

AS IT SEEMS. EACH DAY YOU HAVE A NEW

CHANCE TO BE HAPPY AND BECOME A

BETTER PERSON. GOD MADE US ALL AND

HE GAVE US ALL SOMETHING SPECIAL.

YOU ARE VERY SPECIAL. DID YOU KNOW,

DID YOU?

DID YOU KNOW, THAT NOBODY IS
BETTER THAN YOU AND GOD MADE YOU
SPECIAL. FIND SOMETHING THAT YOU
ENJOY DOING AND BECOME THE BEST AT
IT. NO ONE IS BETTER THAN YOU. YOU ARE
THE BEST. DID YOU KNOW, DID YOU?

DID YOU KNOW, TO ALWAYS KEEP

YOUR WORD GOOD. WHEN YOU TELL

SOMEONE YOU ARE GOING TO DO

SOMETHING, DO IT. YOU WILL BE

RESPECTED. YOU ARE ONLY AS GOOD

AS YOUR WORD. DID YOU KNOW, DID YOU?

THANK YOU BOYS AND GIRLS FOR

YOUR TIME. I HOPE I SAID SOMETHING

THAT CAN HELP YOU. THERE'S NO SUCH

THING AS A STUPID QUESTION, DON'T

WORRY ABOUT WHAT OTHERS THINK,

ASK YOUR QUESTION AND ALWAYS KNOW

THAT YOU ARE SMART, SPECIAL AND GREAT.

"DID YOU KNOW" "DID YOU"?

THE END !!!